SHOOTING WAR

WRITTEN BY ANTHONY LAPPÉ
ILLUSTRATED BY DAN GOLDMAN

WEIDENFELD & NICOLSON
LONDON

FIRST PUBLISHED IN GREAT BRITAIN IN 2007
BY WEIDENFELD & NICOLSON

1 3 5 7 9 10 8 6 4 2

A CIP CATALOGUE RECORD FOR THIS BOOK IS AVAILABLE FROM THE BRITISH LIBRARY

ISBN- 978 0 297 85274 2

PRINTED IN GREAT BRITAIN BY BUTLER & TANNER, FROME AND LONDON

WEIDENFELD & NICOLSON
AN IMPRINT OF THE ORION PUBLISHING GROUP
ORION HOUSE, 5 UPPER ST MARTIN'S LANE, LONDON WC2H 9EA
WWW.ORIONBOOKS.CO.UK

FOR CLARICE AND LILLI

WITHOUT WHOM...

SIGNAL

NEW YORK MAYOR RASIEJ HAS ORDERED MARTIAL LAW. AT AROUND 2:15 LOCAL TIME, SYRIAN BORN ALI MASAB AL-TAHERI WALKED INTO A STARBUCKS IN THE FASHIONABLE WILLIAMSBURG SECTION OF BROOKLYN AND DETONATED A POWERFUL HOMEMADE EXPLOSIVE DEVICE. AT THAT SAME MOMENT, A BLOGGER NAMED JIMMY BURNS HAPPENED TO BE BROADCASTING A LIVE VIDEO FEED TO HIS POPULAR LEFT-WING WEB SITE.

BURNS CAPTURED THESE INCREDIBLE PICTURES, INCLUDING AL-TAHERI ENTERING THE STARBUCKS AND THE DEVASTATING EXPLOSION SECONDS LATER.

WITHIN MINUTES, BURNS' VIDEO WAS STREAMING LIVE EXCLUSIVELY HERE ON GLOBAL. THE EXTRAORDINARY VIDEO HELPED AUTHORITIES IDENTIFY AL-TAHERI AND LOCATE HIS TERROR CELL.

WITHIN THE HOUR, HOMELAND SECURITY AGENTS RAIDED A QUEENS WAREHOUSE AND ARRESTED THREE INDIVIDUALS--

--FOILING WHAT THEY SAY WAS A PLANNED SECOND ATTACK AT A MANHATTAN CHILI'S RESTAURANT.

IT'S THE SECOND TERRORIST ATTACK ON AMERICAN SOIL SINCE PRESIDENT MCCAIN TOOK OFFICE, AND THE NATION IS ON FULL ALERT.

JIMMY BURNS LIVE IN STUDIO

IT'S BEEN A DRAMATIC DAY HERE IN NEW YORK, AND AN INCREDIBLE DAY FOR ONE YOUNG BLOGGER.

JIMMY BURNS, TELL US WHAT HAPPENED.

ELTON JOHN 1947-2011

IN THE STUDIO: BROOKLYN BLOGGER JIMMY BURNS

NEXT: WHEN YOUR CHILD IS HIDING A KORAN

TERROR LEV

MAY 16. 2011 / Less humid with clouds and sun, 105°

Blogger: Bite Me, Media Whores
File Under Jimmy Burns HOT

Between his rugged good looks and those bedroom eyes, what self-respecting newsie wouldn't have a Jimmy Burns wallpaper on his desktop? I mean, come on girls! Couldn't we all use some honesty coming out of our big mouths?

1024x860
HD

"What's his problem

THE FUCKED UP THING WAS:

BL

BOI

Can Andre 3000 Fill I

LARRY KING LIVE with JIMMY BURNS: IF CITIZENS ARE .

ED

NUPS AND DOWNS: TOM CRUISE, MARY-KATE OLSEN CALL IT QUITS

**The Grups
5 Years Later –
Why So Grumpy?**

**Work Begins at
Ground Zero**

**James Cramer
Declares Bankruptcy
(Loudly!)**

MAY 15, 2011

Jimmy Burns,
the "hero of Grand Street"

THE
MORE ANGRY I
GOT, THE MORE
PEOPLE SEEMED TO
LIKE IT.

LEFTY
GGER
GOES
KERS

n John's Shoes?

BURNS, BABY,
BURNS

How the v-blogger who
captured the Starbucks
suicide bombing is
changing the face of news

**When Did
Staten Island
Become
*So Cool?***

RNALISTS, WHO WILL BE THE AUDIENCE?

I GUESS I SHOULD HAVE THOUGHT IT OVER A *LITTLE* LONGER BEFORE I AGREED.

ON THE SPOT. TO A THREE-YEAR CONTRACT.

BUT THAT ASSHOLE WAS RIGHT ABOUT A COUPLE THINGS. NOT ALL THE *DIME STORE HEGEL,* BUT THE PART ABOUT MY STUPID BLOG. IT WASN'T CHANGING SHIT.

I HAD EVERY INDYMEDIA CHICK FROM OREGON TO RED HOOK ON MY JOCK. BUT WHAT DID I HAVE TO SHOW FOR IT? WAS SAM WALTON SPINNING IN HIS GRAVE BECAUSE I HAD A SHINY NEW WEBCAM?

I WAS *BROKE.* I HAD NO MEDICAL INSURANCE. NO APARTMENT. NO COMPUTER. AND THE BLOW DID SUCK EVER SINCE THE REBELS TOOK BOGOTA.

MISTER JIMMY, WE MUST GO. WE CAN NO LONGER HOLD THIS POSITION.

MISTER JIMMY, PLEASE...

THE TRUTH WAS, HE WAS RIGHT ABOUT ANOTHER THING.

I DID NEED THE ACTION. I COULDN'T SHAKE THE RUSH. IT WAS LIKE NOTHING I HAD EVER FELT.

SO HERE I AM. LIVE AND DIRECT FROM BEAUTIFUL DOWNTOWN BAGDAD'S. THE WORST FUCKING PLACE ON ALL OF MOHAMMED'S GOOD GREEN EARTH. AND YOU DON'T KNOW THE HALF OF IT.

SH!

DO YOU HEAR...?

MORTAR, MISTER JIMMY!!

MISTER JIMMY!!

LATEST: THAMES BARRIER BREAKS, LONDON FLOODS...GLOBAL WARMING BLAMED

JIMMY BURNS

Jimmy is currently on assignment for the *GLOBAL NEWS* network as embedded vlog correspondent in Baghdad.

Live sat-cam feed here:
feed.globalnews.com/burns

VLOG ARCHIVE:

Corporate Takeover of America series:

Part 19: Eminent Domain Disasters

Part 18: Your DNA, Their $

Part 17: ChoicePoint: They're back

INTO THE BELLY OF THE BEAST

I picked a brilliant time to head into the belly of the beast. Back home, the oil crisis is just hitting its crescendo. After the U.S. and Israel hit Iran's nuke plants, the mullahs teamed up with the Islamic junta in Nigeria and Chavez in Venezuela to cut off oil to the West. The Saudis' oil facilities were under near daily attack. Gas hit $8 a gallon and the U.S. economy spiraled into recession.

Everyone, left, right, and middle, is screaming to get out of Iraq. But McCain appears trapped. The "enduring bases" were built to *endure*. Too much blood has been spilt to give it all away now, the hawks sqawked like tone-deaf parrots.

The oil fields in the north are still under the control of our last friends east of Jericho — the Kurds. But the rest of the country is beyond Thunderdome.

In '09, a desperate McCain disbanded the Interior Ministry and purged the army of Shia extremists. The army was reconstituted with our old allies, the Baathists, whose leadership in the insurgency had been overtaken by foreign jihadists.

It was a bold move. There weren't many "secular nationalists," as McCain liked to call them, left — alive. The 10,000 American troops still in country are the most battle-hardened, ruthless mothers the Pentagon could muster. But even with the gloves off, they can't stem the bloodletting.

In Baghdad, a DMZ barely puts a dent in the ethnic cleansing of the city's last mixed 'hoods. In the western badlands, Al Qaeda and its competitors battle for supremacy.

ALLIES LINKS

Guerrilla News Network

TalkingPoints Memo

Information Clearing House

Crooks and Liars

Sploid

Huffington Post

Gawker

Metafilter

Antiwar

Truthout

War in Context

DailyKos

Treehugger

Show Me the War

Iraq & Afghanistan Veterans of America

ACT-I-VATE

Antiwar

Wonkette

Guardian

The Nation

Doc Searls

Village Voice

AlterNet

Entertainment Weekly

Independent Propaganda

Rolling Stone

AND IN THE SOUTH, THE SHIA MILITIAS ARE STILL FIGHTING AMONGST THEMSELVES FOR CONTROL OF THE SOUTHERN FIELDS WITH A FEROCITY RESERVED FOR INTRA-FRATERNAL SPATS.

GLOBAL

RUMOR IS THE IRANIANS ARE INCHING THEIR WAY NORTH FOR THE GREAT SHOWDOWN ALL THE JESUS FREAKS AND JIHAD-HEADS HAVE BEEN WAITING FOR. IT IS LOOKING MORE AND MORE LIKE SAIGON '75 EVERY DAY.

EITHER THAT, OR JUDGMENT DAY.

THE MOST DANGEROUS THING I EVER DID BACK IN NEW YORK WAS ▮ FUCK THAT TATTED-OUT CHICK I MET AT CHERRY TAVERN WITHOUT A DOME.

NOW EVERYWHERE I GO PEOPLE ARE DYING. THE TWO JOURNAL-ISTS WHO ▮ DIED IN THE CRASH HAD COVERED 13 WARS BETWEEN THE TWO OF THEM. THE OLD DUDE TOLD ME HE AND HIS WIFE JUST HA▮ ▮EIR FIRST KID, AND HE WAS ▮▮PING THIS WAS HIS LAST WAR. ▮WO HOURS LATER WE FACE PLANT INTO THE DESERT. AND I'M THE ONLY ONE TO COME OUT ALIVE.

THEN I GET SHANGHAIED INTO BEING THE PROPAGANDA BITCH FOR SOME MURDEROUS CHE WANNABE WHO ACTUALLY MADE SOME ▮OLID POLITICAL POINTS, BEFOR▮ ▮HIS BOY LOPPED SOME POOR FUCK'S HEAD OFF.

I DON'T THINK I'M *CUT OUT* FOR THIS SHIT..

I REALLY DON'▮

DIEBOLD MULTISPECTRAL SECURITY CHECKPOINT MDX-4123

SCANNING...

ENTRY GRANTED

NICE GIRL. CLEAN GIRL.

TEN U.S. DOLLARS. YOU WANT?

LIVE

ETERNAL
G
VIGILANCE
GLOBAL TELEVISON

BREAKING NEWS

ETERNAL
G
VIGILANCE

U.N. PEACEKEEPER
HELICOPTER SHOT DOWN

EXCLUSIVE LIVE COVERAGE ONLY ON GLOBAL NEWS

WHAT'S YOUR PLAN?

OUR PLAN IS TO SURVIVE - AS IT HAS ALWAYS BEEN.

BEFORE THE IMPERIALIST INVASION, WE WERE THE ONES SPEAKING THE LOUDEST AGAINST SADDAM. BUT YOUR SO-CALLED PEACE ACTIVISTS NEVER SAW FIT TO SPEAK WITH US WHEN THEY CAME ON THEIR "ANTIWAR" MISSIONS.

THEY WERE LED BY THE BAATHIES LIKE DOGS ON LEASHES. WHEN GENERAL POWELL TOLD HIS LIES TO THE UN, WE WARNED THE PEACE-LOVING ARABS THAT THE CHOICE BETWEEN THREE FASCISMS AWAITED US - IMPERIALIST, BAATHIST, AND RELIGIOUS FANATIC.

YOU SEE, WE WERE THE ONLY TRUE HOPE FOR A SECULAR, DEMOCRATIC IRAQ. BUT AFTER THE IN-VASION, IT WAS THE SHEIKS THAT YOUR GOV-ERNMENT GAVE THE POWER. NOW THE MULLAHS IN TEHRAN CONTROL THE SOUTHERN FIELDS.

THE WAHABI AND BAATHIE MILITIAS FIGHT FOR CON-TROL OF THE MIDDLE, THE KURDS WITH HELP FROM THEIR ZIONIST INFILTRATORS, PROTECT THEIR KINGDOM IN THE NORTH LIKE HAWKS, AND YOUR ARMY TRIES TO HOLD ONTO WHATEVER SCRAPS YOU CAN.

THE RESULT IS IRAQ IS NO MORE.

THE GREAT CAPITALISM EXPERIMENT IS DYING HERE IN THE CRADLE OF CIVILIZATION.

IT IS ONE OF HISTORY'S GREAT IRONIES, NO?

MARX IS DEAD, YES. BUT IN-STEAD YOU GIVE US HOBBES.

WHICH WOULD YOU PREFER?

THREE WEEKS LATER

YORK

Jimmy Burns
can't get it up for
Global News

Fear of a Suitcase Nuke:
Are You Freaked Out Yet?

Upper East Side's Designer
DNA Underground

CRASH AND
BURN

How Brooklyn's
most famous
blogger lost his
mojo in Baghdad
by Gabby Petropoulos

NEW YORK CITY

U.S. OUT OF:
IRAQ
AFGHANISTAN MALI
IRAN COLOMBIA ALGERIA
INDONESIA
PHILIPPINES PAKISTAN
UZBEKISTAN
CUBA TURKEY AUSTRALIA

INFIDEL
massacre

INFIDEL
massacre

How Brooklyn's most famous blogger lost his mojo in Baghdad
Crash & Burn

by **Gabby Petropoulos**

It's 9:15 AM and the dingy restaurant of the W Hotel Baghdad is nearly empty.

Three South African mercenaries are barking death threats into a sat-phone at some unlucky soul who owes them money. Dan Rather is picking at his eggs like they are infected with ebola. A stylishly disheveled young American man and a plain but pretty Iraqi woman in a headscarf are huddled conspiratorially over coffee. It's blogger-turned-war correspondent Jimmy Burns and his producer, Sameera al Burkari. The day's assignment has just come in from their boss in New York, Global News' famously combative executive producer Dan Newfeld. But Burns isn't having any of it.

"Fuck New York," he announces. "And fuck Newfeld." — Burns has his own idea.

"Fuck New York"

It is classic Burns — putting his own political agenda ahead of sound news judgment. And like most of what he's done since he arrived in Baghdad, the results are disastrous. Burns misses the day's headline, is scooped by CNN, and is nearly fired by an apoplectic Newfeld.

When Jimmy Burns literally burst into our living rooms this May he was a revelation, and for many, a savior. Younger, cuter, and more "real" than CNN's scion of a designer jean fortune, Burns personified outrage. He perfectly captured the anti-Big Media zeitgeist that swept the country last summer, killing off the broadcast networks' venerable evening newscasts, and nearly bankrupting several cable networks' news divisions. Burns appeared to be the antidote to a business that had long since embraced entertainment values over substance. It didn't hurt that Burns had impeccable populist street cred. He was the first blogger to make the jump from the obscurity of the web to fully-fledged war-on-terror correspondent. But it wasn't just the novelty of his career path. There was something about him that captured our imaginations, and our hearts. He was our blogger. Burns would redeem us.

Finally, there was a reporter who could explain what was really happening in that murky Mad Max cauldron of hate that was still taking the lives of our countrymen and women long after we'd all gone back to buying Blahniks and watching football (as if we ever stopped). But, alas, Burns has been a bust. His channel's ratings have sunk to their lowest ever and his Q rating, the closely guarded indicator of a television personality's familiarity and appeal, is allegedly scraping rock bottom. Burns' failures to perform under pressure in Baghdad has left many media insiders wondering whether Newfeld himself is one five-Foster lunch away from a red slip.

LATEST: WEST AFRICAN OIL WAR WORSENS. ANGOLAN TROOPS TAKE HEAVY LOSSES

JIMMY BURNS

Jimmy is currently on assignment for the *GLOBAL NEWS* network as embedded vlog correspondent in Baghdad.

Live sat-cam feed here:
feed.globalnews.com/burns

VLOG ARCHIVE:

Corporate Takeover of America series:

Part 19: Eminent Domain Disasters

Part 18: Your DNA, Their $

Part 17: ChoicePoint: They're back

THE HONEYMOON IS OVER

Had another nightmare last night. This time my mother made a cameo. Don't ask.

I've been here five months, and everything still feels so alien. Nothing I do seems to go right. The honeymoon is over, kids. Sometimes I don't want to get out of bed in the morning, let alone risk my neck hitting the streets to report on what blew up that day. I don't know if anything I do here makes a smidgen of difference in how you back home understand this conflict.

It's one thing to be brave. It's another thing altogether to try to make sense of centuries-old conflicts when you don't even speak the language or understand the religion, let alone the dozen or so factions with thousands of competing individuals intent on slaughtering each other like animals on a daily basis.

It's really hard to describe how much Baghdad sucks. If the insurgents don't get you, the heat, the pollution, or the kebab that hits your colon like an IED, will. Even the Iraqis are complaining the weather has turned downright Dante-esque. It got to 132 Fahrenheit the other day.

Monster flash sandstorms have been wreaking havoc on oil facilities and American aircraft across the country. An army weather guy told me he had no doubt they are connected to the rising ocean temps that are making this year's hurricane and monsoon season so nasty.

The blast windows keep out most of the sound from my room at night. But the thud of mortars and the crack of gunfire still keep me up. Just to fuck with us, Apaches sometimes buzz the high floors of the hotel in the ass crack of the morning. Your room rattles as if you're inside a giant vibrator.

I wish I could report the political situation is getting any better, but the new government (that's number 11 if you're counting) is AWOL. The PM hasn't left his bunker for weeks. No one has actually seen the Minister of the Interior — he won't allow his face to be photographed. Death squads continue to operate with impunity. As one journalist told me, "Iraq is Salvador without the surf." The problem is that trying to verify any of it is near impossible. Ever since the Pentagon got busted enlisting Pixar to create al-Zaraqwi's successor out of 0s and 1s, getting straight answers out of the military is like asking James Frey what he learned in prison.

And, no, I still have nothing on the Sword of Mohammed.

(MORE)

ALLIES LINKS

Guerrilla News Network

TalkingPoints Memo

Information Clearing House

Crooks and Liars

Sploid

Huffington Post

Gawker

Metafilter

Antiwar

Truthout

War in Context

DailyKos

Treehugger

Show Me the War

Iraq & Afghanistan Veterans of America

ACT-I-VATE

Antiwar

Wonkette

Guardian

The Nation

Doc Searls

Village Voice

AlterNet

Entertainment Weekly

Independent Propaganda

Rolling Stone

Live sat-cam feed here:
feed.globalnews.com/burns

VLOG ARCHIVE:

Corporate Takeover of America series:

Part 19: Eminent Domain Disasters

Part 18: Your DNA, Their $

Part 17: ChoicePoint: They're back

Part 16: Net Neutrality: Moot?

SEE ALL >

Despite the fact Abu Adallah somehow considers me a soul brother. Scary, I know.

Lastly, thanks for your emails. Kiki77 in Laguna Beach writes: "My friends and I at the skate shop argue about you all the time. They say you're a sell out for working for Global News. I try to tell them you're just infiltrating the system. But I want to know what you say. Why did you take the job?"

Kiki & Co.: This gig is a chance to see things firsthand and to try and show all Americans what's going down in their name.

There's only four American correspondents left here, and one of them is Dan Rather. BTW, thanks for the Spring Break slideshow. It, um, sure helped pass the time between blackouts.

http://burnbabyburn.com

LATEST: IN GOD WE TRUST: U.S. CLAIMS GLOBAL ORBIT DEFENDER (GOD) PLATFORM FULLY OPERATIONAL BY 2012

JIMMY BURNS

Jimmy is currently on assignment for the *GLOBAL NEWS* network as embedded vlog correspondent in Baghdad.

Live sat-cam feed here: *feed.globalnews.com/burns*

VLOG ARCHIVE:

Corporate Takeover of America series:

Part 19: Eminent Domain Disasters

Part 18: Your DNA, Their $

Part 17: ChoicePoint: They're back

DAMAGE

Being a war correspondent eats away at your soul. It happens slowly.

First, the guns, the bombs, and the explosions are exciting. Even the death is a rush. You dodged it. You've tricked the reaper. You must be special. You've never felt more alive. Then the blood finds its way into your dreams.

You find your mind wandering into the darkness at night as you lie in your bed. You replay the carnage over and over. The more you try to think about puppies and waterfalls and eating a slice of pizza on Bedford with your best friend Geno, the more your mind rebels and reminds you of the half a torso of a little boy you almost stepped on last Tuesday. Or the street full of kids you watched get gunned down in cold blood. Then the carnage bleeds all the way into your waking hours. You see it on the blank walls, in our food, in your reflection in the mirror. Doctors call it PTSD — post-traumatic stress disorder. I call it being human. If this shit doesn't fuck you up then you should see a doctor because you're a sociopath.

You cover it up, because you have to. You cover up a lot of things, because you have to — to survive.

Your humble correspondent out.

ALLIES LINKS

Guerrilla News Network

TalkingPoints Memo

Information Clearing House

Crooks and Liars

Sploid

Huffington Post

Gawker

Metafilter

Antiwar

Truthout

War in Context

DailyKos

Treehugger

Show Me the War

Iraq & Afghanistan Veterans of America

ACT-I-VATE

Antiwar

Wonkette

Guardian

The Nation

Doc Searls

Village Voice

AlterNet

Entertainment Weekly

Independent Propaganda

Rolling Stone

JIMMY, WHO ARE THESE MEN?

I'M WATCHING YOU.

HE'S ALWAYS WATCHING ME.

I'M HAPPY TO SEE YOU MADE IT TO BAGHDAD.

JIMMY, HURRY. THE SANDSTORM!

SAMEERA, TELL ME YOU GOT THAT ON TAPE.

NO.

HOLD UP, WE WERE JUST SMACK IN THE MIDDLE OF A SHOOT-OUT BETWEEN THE MOST WANTED TERRORIST IN IRAQ AND THE CRAZIEST COMMANDER IN THE U.S. ARMY, AND WE GOT NOTHING?

THE MANIAC WITH THE 9MM TO MY HEAD MADE IT A LITTLE TRICKY. SO PLEASE, JIMMY BURNS, SHUT THE FUCK UP AND DRIVE...

SHIA INSURGENTS HAVE LAUNCHED A SERIES OF MAJOR ATTACKS ACROSS IRAQ TODAY, CATCHING AMERICAN AND IRAQI NATIONALIST FORCES OFF-GUARD.

THE AMERICAN PROTECTED GREEN ZONE IS IN CHAOS WHERE A NON-STOP BARRAGE OF MORTAR AND ROCKET ATTACKS HAS CAUSED AN UNKNOWN NUMBER OF CASUALTIES SINCE EARLY THIS MORNING LOCAL TIME.

THE ATTACK COMES ON THE HEELS OF YESTERDAY'S ASSASSINATION OF THE U.S. AMBASSADOR TO IRAQ. THE U.S. MILITARY HAS ORDERED THE EVACUATION OF NON-ESSENTIAL PERSONNEL FROM THE GREEN ZONE, AND HAS TEMPORARILY SUSPENDED THE JOURNALIST EMBED PROGRAM.

ALL MEDIA PERSONNEL HAVE BEEN CONFINED TO THEIR HOTELS FOR THEIR OWN SAFETY, ACCORDING TO A STATE-MENT FROM THE GREEN ZONE PRESS OFFICE.

THEY ARE CALLING IT IRAQ'S TET OFFENSIVE.

19%: MCCAIN APPROVAL RATINGS HIT ALL-TIME LOW GLOBAL NE

PRESIDENT MCCAIN HAS CALLED FOR ANOTHER 10,000 AMERICAN TROOPS TO BE MOBILIZED TO AID NATIONALIST FORCES.

AMERICAN INTELLIGENCE SOURCES TELL GLOBAL NEWS THAT THEY BELIEVE IRAN IS SUPPLY-ING ARMS, MILITARY HARDWARE, AND EVEN ELITE COMMANDO TROOPS FOR THE INSURGENT OFFENSIVE AND MAY HAVE HAD A HAND IN YESTERDAY'S ASSASSINATION.

PRESIDENT MCCAIN HAS CALLED ON IRAN TO WITHDRAW ITS SUPPORT OR FACE MASSIVE RETALIATION. FOR MORE ON THIS TENSE SITUATION, WE GO TO PETER WILLIAMS AT THE PENTAGON...

NEWS YOUR 24-HOURS TERROR NEWS SOURCE 19%: MCCAIN APPROVAL RATINGS HIT ALL-TIME LOW

DON'T SHOOT! DON'T SHOOT!

TV GOOD. TV GOOD. WE GO.

GLOBAL

AS THE WORST VIOLENCE SINCE 2009 RAGES ACROSS IRAQ TODAY, TERRORISTS STEPPED UP THEIR ATTACKS ACROSS THE GLOBE. SUICIDE BOMBERS STRUCK AGAIN IN EUROPE, WITH DEADLY RESULTS.

TWO POWERFUL BOMBS WENT OFF IN THE SUBWAYS OF LONDON AND MADRID, KILLING 56 AND WOUNDING HUNDREDS.

COORDINATED ATTACK ON GULF OF MEXICO OIL RIG
BREAKING NEWS
STOX REAX: DOW DOWN 7%. NASDAQ DOWN 3.4%. NIKKEI DOWN 6.4%

IN THE GULF OF MEXICO, A COORDINATED SUICIDE BOMB ATTACK BY THREE SMALL PLANES LOADED WITH EXPLOSIVES DESTROYED THREE OF AMERICA'S MOST PRODUCTIVE OIL DRILLING RIGS, KILLING 23, WOUNDING HUNDREDS MORE, AND SHUTTING DOWN AMERICA'S DRILLING CAPABILITIES IN THE GULF.

ALMOST ALL AREAS OF AMERICA'S OIL INDUSTRY WERE SHUT DOWN AND PUT ON HIGH ALERT, CUTTING OFF NEARLY 25% OF THE NATION'S OIL SUPPLY, DRIVING OIL PRICES TO AN ALL-TIME HIGH OF $150 A BARREL. IN THE FEW METROPOLITAN AREAS WHERE YOU COULD BUY IT, GAS IS NOW $15 A GALLON.

WHITE HOUSE SOURCES TELL CNN THEY BELIEVE CUBA WAS USED AS A LAUNCHING POINT FOR THE ATTACKS --

LIVE

-- FURTHER PUTTING PRESSURE ON PRESIDENT MCCAIN TO TAKE ACTION AGAINST THE RAUL CASTRO GOVERNMENT.

FINALLY, THE SPIRALING VIOLENCE BETWEEN ISRAELI DEFENSE FORCES AND PALESTINIAN MILITANTS IN JERUSALEM SPREAD TO THE DOME OF THE ROCK LATE TODAY. THERE ARE REPORTS OF GUNFIRE HITTING THE SACRED MUSLIM TEMPLE, CAUSING WIDESPREAD RIOTS ACROSS THE ISLAMIC WORLD. HERE IN THE U.S., AMERICAN EVANGELICAL LEADERS ISSUED A STATEMENT CALLING THE DOME OF THE ROCK VIOLENCE PROOF THAT ALL CHRISTIANS SHOULD READY THEMSELVES FOR THE SECOND COMING OF THEIR SAVIOR, JESUS CHRIST.

SNAP OUT OF IT. WHAT IS WRONG WITH YOU?

DON'T YOU SEE SAMEERA. WE'RE NOT MAKING IT OFF THIS ROOF. IT'S OVER...

GET IT TOGETHER.

I'M UPLOADING...

FINE. YOU WANT SOMETHING? UPLOAD THIS.

UPLOADING TO FEED.GLOBALNEWS.COM/BURNS
BUFFERING AT 36.8%...   09:54:78:03

BATT

SIGNAL

MY NAME IS JIMMY BURNS. I'M A LIAR, A FAKE, A FRAUD.

YOU THINK YOU KNOW MY STORY...

ETERNAL
G
VIGILANCE

14:23:47
10.28.11

A BIG MAC?

I LIKE TO EAT THE FOOD OF MY ENEMY BEFORE BATTLE. IT HELPS ME UNDERSTAND THEM.

THIS BURGER MAKES ME FEEL SATED YET VAGUELY DISGUSTED WITH MYSELF.

WHAT I IMAGINE IT FEELS LIKE TO BE AMERICAN EVERYDAY.

NOT FAR OFF.

WHY MAKE IT LOOK LIKE IRAN IS BEHIND ALL OF THIS?

DON'T YOU WANT THE CREDIT?

THE MULLAHS.

THEY ARE OUR MOVEMENT'S GREATEST ENEMY.

ALRIGHT MEN, WE'RE GOING TO DO THIS THE HARD WAY.

HOTEL BAGHDAD

MED ONE

MED ONE

My Videos - Favorites - Playlists - Inbox - Subs

Video Upload (Step 2 of 2)

File: /SD20GB/Mogadishu.mpg5   Browse...

Maximum fil...

Max file size: 100 MB. Ma...

Do not upload copyri...
Use.

Broad...

...hd...ct list.

...c videos...sic concerts, or commercials ...consist entirely of content you created

...deo," you are representing that this video does not violate ...of Use and that you own all copyrights in this video or have

Record videos directly from
your desktop camera!

Try it now

Upload videos directly from
your mobile phone!

Set up your preferences

ONE WEEK AFTER AMERICAN FORCES IN IRAQ REPELLED A MAJOR ASSAULT BY SLAIN TERRORIST LEADER ABU ADALLAH, PRESIDENT MCCAIN MADE A SHOCKING ANNOUNCEMENT.

MCCAIN: AUTUMN OF A HERO

BREAKING NEWS

MCCAIN SHOCKER: 'I WILL NOT RUN' • SON STILL MISSING • DELAY: 'MCCAIN TRAITOR TO

EARLIER TODAY, THE PRESIDENT ANNOUNCED HE WOULD NOT SEEK RE-ELECTION AS THE REPUBLI-CAN NOMINEE IN 2012. WHITE HOUSE SOURCES TELL CNN THAT THE PRESIDENT HAD BECOME INCREASINGLY DESPONDENT OVER HIS SON'S ONGOING ABDUCTION AND THAT HE WAS DISTRAUGHT BY FRESH ALLEGATIONS OF AMERICAN WAR CRIMES.

THE IMAGES OF AN AMERICAN LT. COL. EXECUTING AN ELDERLY IRAQI WOMAN ON AN IRAQI STREET AND AMERICAN REMOTE CONTROLLED ROBOTS KILLING UNARMED CIVILIANS UPLOADED TO YOUTUBE BY FORMER GLOBAL NEWS CORRESPONDENT JIMMY BURNS WERE SAID TO HAVE ESPECIALLY DISTURBED THE VIETNAM VETERAN CHIEF EXECUTIVE.

THE ANNOUNCEMENT HAS LEFT THE NATION STUNNED. MANY COMMENTATORS COMPARED MCCAIN'S DEMEANOR TO A DEFEATED-

LOOKING PRESIDENT LYNDON JOHNSON WHO SHOCKED THE NATION IN MARCH 1968 WHEN HE ANNOUNCED HE WOULD NOT SEEK A SECOND TERM IN OFFICE. MUCH HAD BEEN MADE ABOUT PRESIDENT MCCAIN'S MENTAL STATE IN THE LAST THREE MONTHS, WITH MANY WHITE HOUSE INSIDERS SAYING HE APPEARED TO BE SHOWING SIGNS OF DEPRESSION.

RUMORS HAVE CIRCULATED OF SESSIONS WITH THERAPISTS AND PRIESTS, AND EVEN AN ADDICTION TO ANTI-DEPRESSANTS. IT IS CLEAR THAT THE LAST THREE YEARS HAS TAKEN ITS TOLL ON THE 75-YEAR-OLD MAN WHO ENDURED MORE THAN FIVE YEARS IN A VIETCONG PRISON TO GO ON TO SERVE ONE TERM IN THE HOUSE OF REPRESENTATIVES AND FOUR TERMS IN THE U.S. SENATE BEFORE BECOMING THE 44TH PRESIDENT OF THE UNITED STATES.

MCCAIN: AUTUMN OF A HERO

BREAKING NEWS

DELAY: 'MCCAIN TRAITOR TO PARTY' • WONKETTE: PREZ

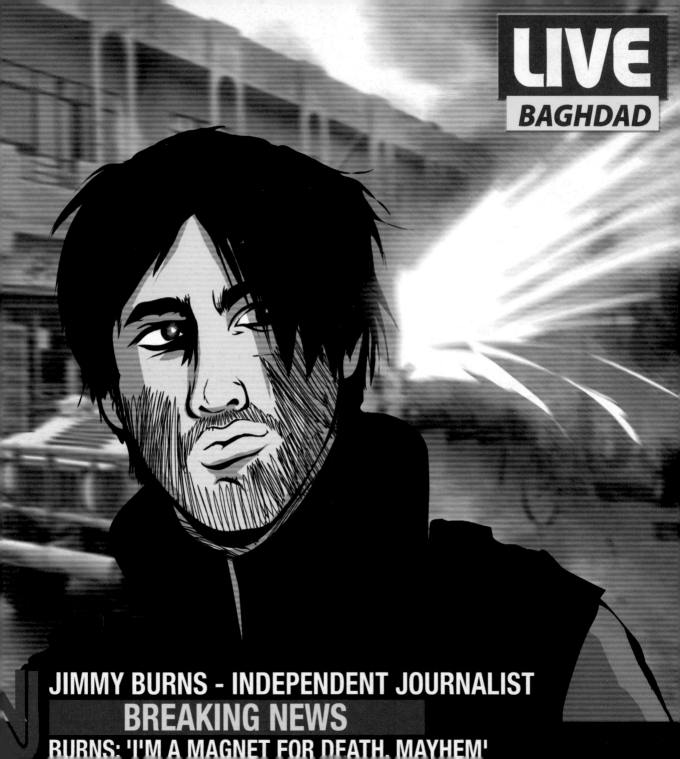

LIVE

BAGHDAD

JIMMY BURNS - INDEPENDENT JOURNALIST
BREAKING NEWS
BURNS: 'I'M A MAGNET FOR DEATH, MAYHEM'

THIS BOOK IS A WORK OF POLITICAL SATIRE. WE HOPE IT GETS YOU THINKING ABOUT SOME BIG QUESTIONS CONCERNING THE MEDIA, THE WAR IN IRAQ, AND AMERICAN FOREIGN POLICY IN GENERAL. WE ALSO HOPE IT MAKES YOU CHUCKLE.

FIRST AND FOREMOST, WE'D LIKE TO THANK THE INTREPID READERS OF SMITH MAGAZINE WHO HELPED MAKE THE ONLINE PREVIEW OF THIS BOOK A WEB PHENOMENON THROUGH THEIR SUPPORT, CONTRIBUTIONS, AND FEEDBACK. ESSENTIAL THANKS TO SMITH PUBLISHER LARRY SMITH FOR SEEING THE FUTURE AND TO TIM BARKOW FOR HELPING US BUILD IT; TO OUR AGENT IAN KLEINERT FOR HIS WISE CONSUL; AND TO JEFF NEWELT FOR CREATING THE CULTURAL PETRI DISH WHERE THIS AND MANY OTHER AMAZING PROJECTS LIVE AND BREED. BUT MOST SIGNIFICANTLY, WE'D LIKE TO EXPRESS OUR DEEPEST GRATITUDE TO OUR EDITOR, JAIME LEVINE, AND HER ASSISTANT TIMOTHY MUCCI FOR THEIR VISION AND GUIDANCE IN HELPING TURN A SCRAPPY ONLINE COMIC INTO A WORK OF LITERATURE.

IN ADDITION, WE'D LIKE TO THANK EVERYONE WHO HELPED SHOOTING WAR SPREAD FAR AND WIDE: HEIDI MACDONALD, JULIAN DIBBELL, BRIAN LAM, CALVIN REID, CHRIS ARRANT, JOE GORDON, RICH JOHNSTON, ANGELA GUNN, BRUCE STERLING, MARK FRAUENFELDER, DENNIS CROWLEY, TIM LEONG, MATT KOELBL, CAMILA VIEGAS-LEE, EDUARDO SIMOES, TERESSA IEZZI, T. CAMPBELL, DAN GILMOR, AND MICHAEL SLENSKE.

FINALLY, NONE OF THIS WOULD BE POSSIBLE WITHOUT THE SUPPORT, INSPIRATION, COLLABORATION, AND ENCOURAGEMENT OF DOUG JAEGER, MARK CREEL, THE HAPPY CORP, LVHRD, BOB MECOY, NICK BERTOZZI, SIMON FRASER, DEAN HASPIEL AND THE REST OF THE ACT-I-VATE CREW, DOUGLAS RUSHKOFF, MARY MAXWELL, PAUL POPE, CHARLES BROWNSTEIN, DJ SPOOKY, ADAM MATTA, RACHEL KRAMER BUSSELL, MICHAEL GESZEL, MILES VANMETER, DANNY FINGEROTH, RYAN ROMAN, ARIEL PALITZ, DAN LANTOWSKI, DOUGLAS LITTLE, MIDTOWN COMICS, FORBIDDEN PLANET, ROCKETSHIP, SAPPORO, SAMSUNG, TOBI ELKIN, JEFF AYERS, VANESSA ARRICO, DANIEL WHITE, KRISTIN JONES, PAUL RIECKHOFF, DAVID ENDERS, PHILLIP ROBERTSON, RICHARD ROWE, MORRIS GOLDMAN, CAROL GOLDMAN, FRANCES MOORE LAPPÉ, ANNA LAPPÉ, AND LAURA THOMAS.

WE WANT TO GRATEFULLY ACKNOWLEDGE THAT PHOTO SOURCES CAME FROM, AMONG OTHER SOURCES, CHRISTIAN PEACEMAKERS TEAMS, THE U.S. GOVERNMENT, AND **BATTLEGROUND: 21 DAYS ON THE EMPIRE'S EDGE.**

SHOOTING WAR WAS DRAWN DIGITALLY USING A WACOM CINTIQ 21UX INTERACTIVE PEN DISPLAY.

SHOOTING WAR WAS ORIGINALLY SERIALIZED ONLINE AT SMITHMAG.NET.

CREATIVE CONSULTANT: JEFF NEWELT

WWW.SHOOTINGWAR.COM
THE FREQUENCY IS COURAGE